HAL LEONARD *MORE* Easy Pop Bass Lines

BASS METHOD

Supplement to Any Bass Method

T0053207

INTRODUCTION

Welcome to *More Easy Pop Bass Lines*, a collection of 20 pop and rock favorites arranged for easy bass. If you're a beginning to intermediate-level bassist, you've come to the right place; these well-known songs will have you playing, reading, and enjoying music in no time!

This book can be used on its own or as a supplement to the *Hal Leonard Bass Method* or any other beginning to intermediate-level bass method. The songs are arranged in order of difficulty. Each bass line is presented in an easy-to-read format—including lyrics to help you follow along and chords for optional accompaniment (by your teacher, if you have one).

ISBN 978-0-634-07353-3

HAL•LEONARD®
CORPORATION

7777 W. BLUEMOUND RD. P.O. BOX 13819 MILWAUKEE, WI 53213

Visit Hal Leonard Online at
www.halleonard.com

SONG STRUCTURE

The songs in this book have different sections, which may or may not include the following:

Intro
This is usually a short instrumental section that "introduces" the song at the beginning.

Verse
This is one of the main sections of a song and conveys most of the storyline. A song usually has several verses, all with the same music but each with different lyrics.

Chorus
This is often the most memorable section of a song. Unlike the verse, the chorus usually has the same lyrics every time it repeats.

Bridge
This section is a break from the rest of the song, often having a very different chord progression and feel.

Solo
This is an instrumental section, often played over the verse or chorus structure.

Outro
Similar to an intro, this section brings the song to an end.

ENDINGS & REPEATS

Many of the songs have some new symbols that you must understand before playing. Each of these represents a different type of ending.

1st and 2nd Endings
These are indicated by brackets and numbers. The first time through a song section, play the first ending and then repeat. The second time through, skip the first ending, and play through the second ending.

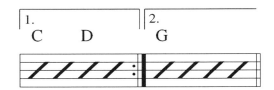

D.S.
This means "Dal Segno" or "from the sign." When you see this abbreviation above the staff, find the sign (𝄋) earlier in the song and resume playing from that point.

al Coda
This means "to the Coda," a concluding section in the song. If you see the words "D.S. al Coda," return to the sign (𝄋) earlier in the song and play until you see the words "To Coda," then skip to the Coda at the end of the song, indicated by the symbol: ⊕.

al Fine
This means "to the end." If you see the words "D.S. al Fine," return to the sign (𝄋) earlier in the song and play until you see the word "Fine."

D.C.
This means "Da Capo" or "from the head." When you see this abbreviation above the staff, return to the beginning (or "head") of the song and resume playing.

CONTENTS

Rock and Roll All Nite

Words and Music by
PAUL STANLEY and GENE SIMMONS

You show us ev-'ry-thing you've got. ___

1. You show us ev-'ry-thing you've got. _____
2. You keep on say-in' you'll be mine for a-while. ___

You keep on danc-in' and the room ___ gets hot.
You're look-in' fan-cy and I like your style.

You drive us wild; _____ we'll drive you cra -
And you drive us wild; _____ we'll drive you cra -

- zy. ___
- zy. ___
You ___ say you wan - na
You ___ show us ev - 'ry -

go for a spin. ___
thing you've ___ got. ___
The par - ty's just be - gun; we'll
Ba - by, ba - by, that's

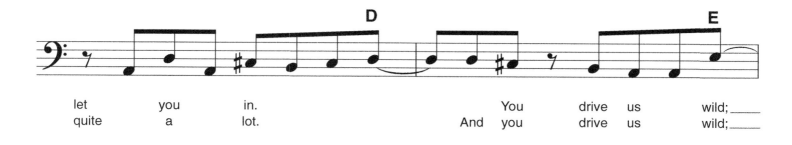

let you in.
quite a lot.
You drive us wild; ___
And you drive us wild; ___

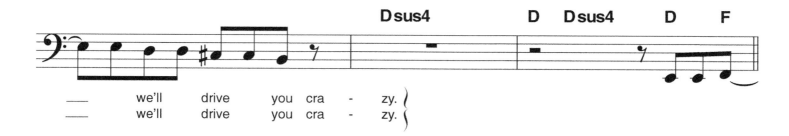

___ we'll drive you cra - zy.
___ we'll drive you cra - zy.

Pre-Chorus

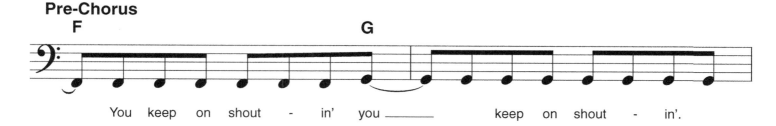

You keep on shout - in' you ___ keep on shout - in'.

Chorus

I ___ wan - na rock and roll ___ all night, ___

and par - ty ev - er - y day.   I   wan - na

rock and   roll __ all   night _____   and par - ty ev - er - y day.

I   wan - na   rock and   roll __ all   night _____   and par - ty ev - er - y day.

I   wan-na rock and roll __ all   night_____   and par - ty ev - er - y day.

and par-ty ev-er-y day.   I   wan - na

Play 5 times and fade

rock and   roll __ all   night _____   and par - ty ev - er - y day.

MESSAGE IN A BOTTLE

Music and Lyrics by
STING

Melody:

Just a cast - a - way, ___

Intro

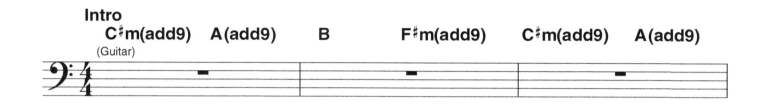

C#m(add9)   A(add9)   B   F#m(add9)   C#m(add9)   A(add9)

(Guitar)

B   F#m(add9) C#m   %Verse   A   B

1. Just   a   cast -
2. A   year ___
3. Walked out   this ___

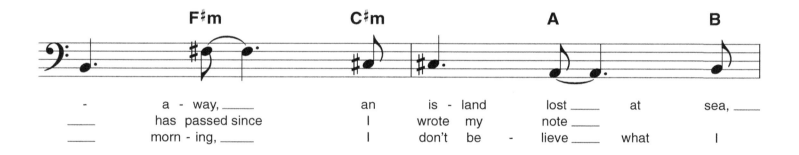

F#m   C#m   A   B

- a - way, ___   an   is - land   lost ___ at   sea, ___
___ has passed since   I   wrote my   note ___
___ morn - ing, ___   I   don't be - lieve ___ what   I

F#m   C#m   A   B   F#m   C#m

___   oh. ___   An - oth - er   lone - ly day, ___
saw,   but I should have known   this right from the
                        a hun - dred bil - lion bot - tles ___

no one   here___ but   me,_____   oh.___   More
start.   Only   hope
washed up   on___ the   shore._____   Seems like I'm

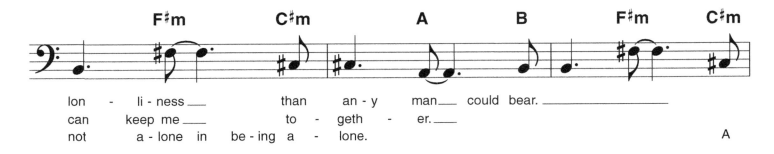

lon - li - ness ___   than   an - y   man___ could   bear._____
can   keep   me ___   to - geth - er.___
not   a - lone in   be - ing a - lone.   A

Res - cue   me _____ be - fore___ I   fall _____ in - to ___ des - pair, ___
Love ___ can   mend ___ your   life ___ but   love _____ can   break ___ your   heart. ___
hun - dred bil - lion   cast - a - ways   look - ing   for___ a   home.

Chorus

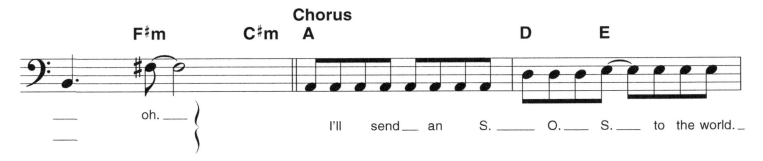

___   oh. ___ }   I'll   send___ an   S. ___ O. ___ S. ___ to the world. __

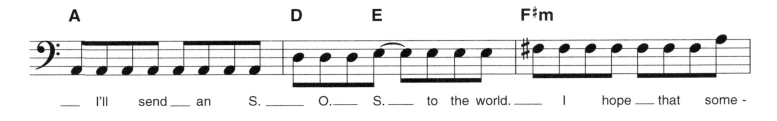

___ I'll   send ___ an   S. ___ O. ___ S. ___ to   the   world. ___   I   hope ___ that   some -

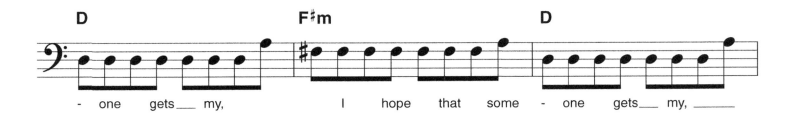

- one   gets ___ my,   I   hope   that   some - one   gets ___ my, _____

F#m — I hope ___ that some - one gets ___ my ___ mes - sage in ___ a bot -

To Coda ⊕

C#m   A — tle, ___ yeah.

C#m   A   F#m [1.] — Mes-sage in ___ a bot - tle, ___ yeah.

[2.] C#m   A

C#m   A   C#m — Mes-sage in ___ a bot - tle, ___ yeah.

A   C#m   A — Mes - sage in ___ a bot - tle, ___ yeah.

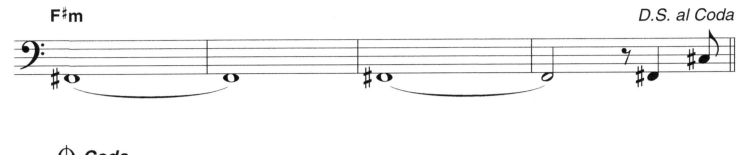

Mes-sage in ___ a bot - tle, ___

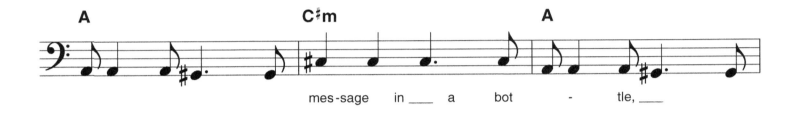

mes-sage in ___ a bot - tle, ___

mes-sage in ___ a bot -

- tle, ___ oh yeah.

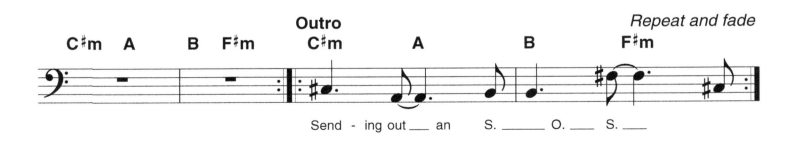

Send - ing out ___ an S. ___ O. ___ S. ___

PARANOID

Words and Music by ANTHONY IOMMI,
JOHN OSBOURNE, WILLIAM WARD and TERENCE BUTLER

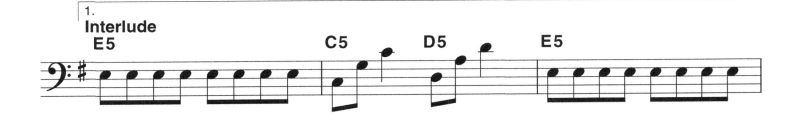

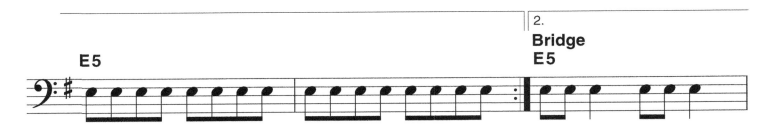

Can you help me   oc - cu - py my

brain?___   Whoa ___ yeah. ___

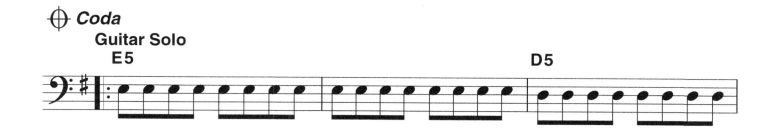

⊕ Coda
Guitar Solo
E5   D5

1., 3.
G5 D5   E5   2., 4.   G5 D5   E5   **Interlude** E5

D5   G5 D5   E5

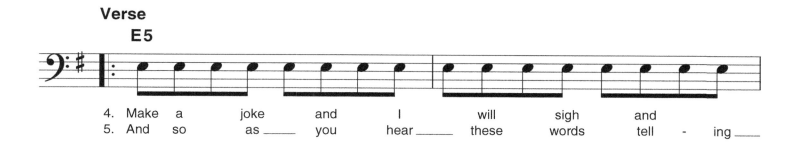

Verse
E5

4. Make   a   joke   and   I   will   sigh   and
5. And   so   as ____ you   hear ____ these   words   tell - ing ____

D5   G5 D5   E5

you will   laugh   and   I ____ will   cry.   Hap-pi - ness   I   can -
____ you   now ____ of ____ my   state;   I   tell   you ____ to   en -

                                      D5

- not   feel ____ and   love   to   me ____ is
- joy   life ____ I   wish   I   could ____ but

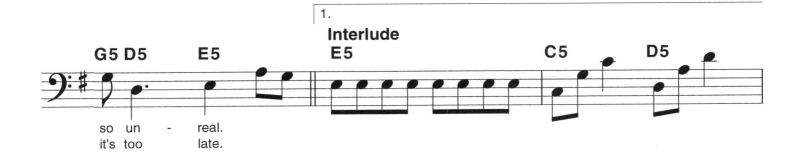

so un - real.
it's too late.

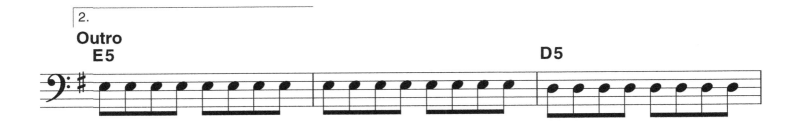

NO EXCUSES

Written by
JERRY CANTRELL

Melody:

It's al - right.____

Intro

(Drums) **4** **Badd4**

Verse
Badd4

1. It's al - right._____ There comes a time.____
2. It's o - kay._____ Had a bad day.____
3. Yeah, it's fine._____ We'll walk down the line.____

____ Got no pa - tience____ to
____ Hands are bruised_____ from
____ Leave our rain,_____ a cold

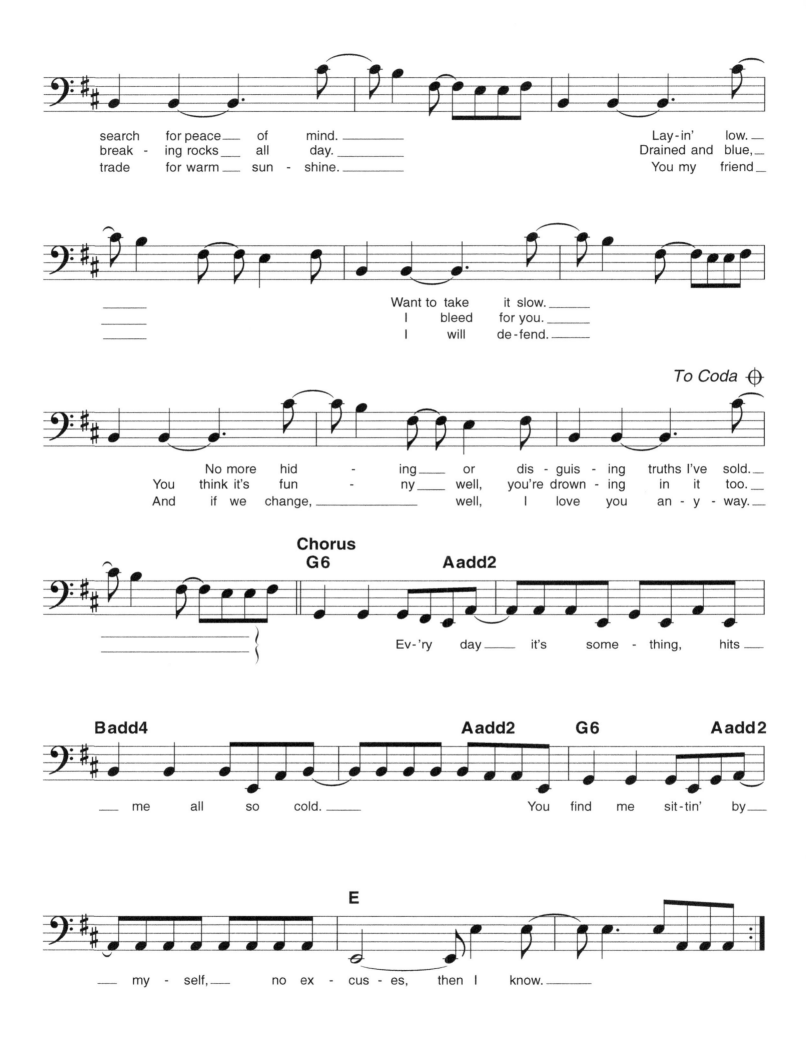

Interlude

Guitar Solo

D.S. al Coda

⊕ *Coda*

Chorus

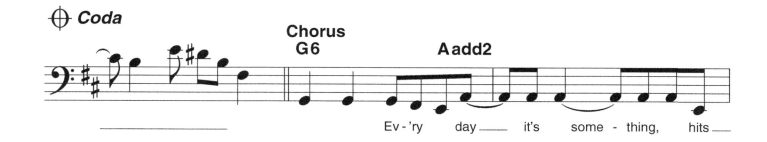

Ev - 'ry day ___ it's some - thing, hits ___

Badd4   **G6**   **Aadd2**

__ me   all   so __ cold. __   You   find   me   sit -tin'   by__

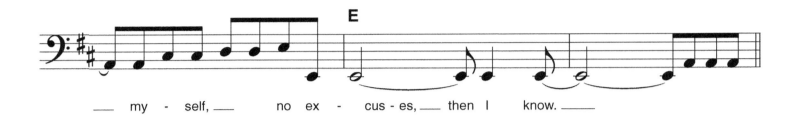

E

__ my - self, __   no   ex - cus - es, __   then   I   know. __

Outro
Badd4

Drums tacet

JAMMING

Words and Music by
BOB MARLEY

Melody:
We're jam-ming.

Intro

Bm7   E9

G   F#m   1.   2.

Ooo, __ yeah.   Al - right.   We're

Chorus

Bm   E7   G   F#m

jam - ming.   I wan - na jam it with you. __

Bm   E7

__ We're jam - ming,   jam - ming,   and I

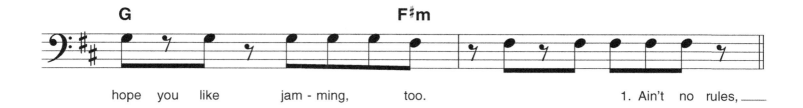

G   F#m

hope you like jam - ming, too.   1. Ain't no rules, __

ain't no vow, we can do it an-y-how.
bul-lets can stop us now, we nei - ther beg nor we won't bow.

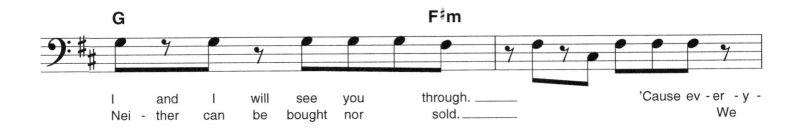

I and I will see you through.
Nei - ther can be bought nor sold.

'Cause ev - er - y-
We

day we pay the price. We are the liv - ing sac - ri - fice,
all de - fend the right, Jah Jah child - ren must u - nite, well,

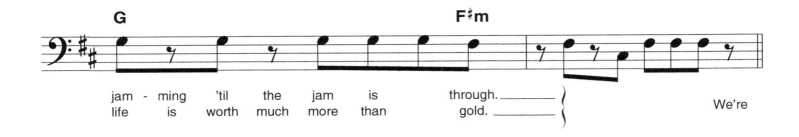

jam - ming 'til the jam is through.
life is worth much more than gold.

We're

Chorus

jam-ming.

To think that jam-ming was a thing of the past.
And we're jam-ming in the name of our Lord.

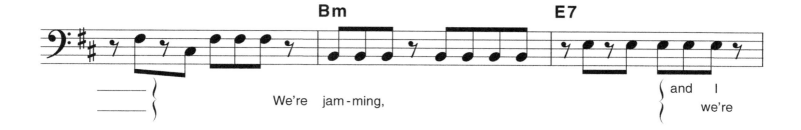

We're jam-ming, and I we're

Interlude

hope this jam is gon-na last. _____ 2. No Ho - ly

jam-ming right straight from yard. _____

Mount Zi - on, ho - ly Mount Zi - on,

Jah sit-teth in Mount Zi - on and rules___ all ___ cre-a-tion. Yeah, we're,

Chorus

we're jam-ming, Bop - chu - wah - wah -

22

STAND BY ME

Words and Music by
BEN E. KING, JERRY LEIBER and MIKE STOLLER

Melody:

When the night —

Intro

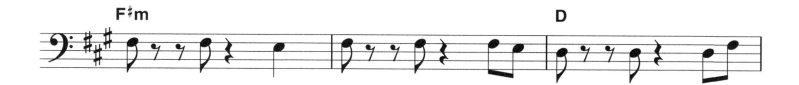

1. When the night —

Verse

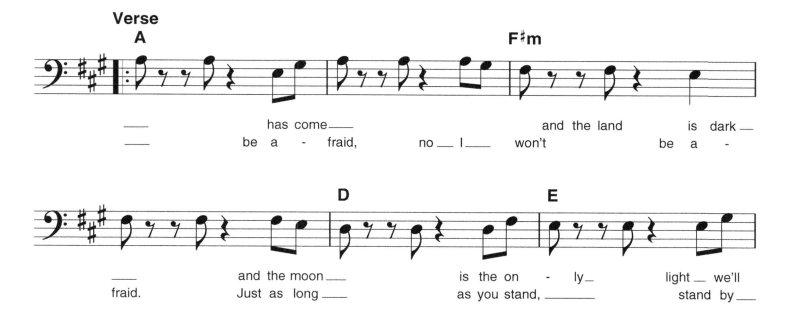

— has come — and the land is dark —

— be a - fraid, no — I — won't be a -

fraid. — and the moon — is the on - ly — light — we'll

Just as long — as you stand, — stand by —

see.

_____ me.   So,

Chorus

stand _____   by   me. _____   Oh, _____   stand _____   by __

me. _____   Oh,   stand, _____   stand by ___ me, _____

stand by ___ me. ___

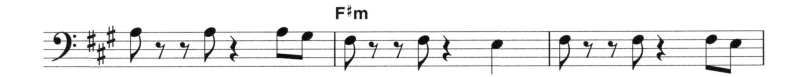

So dar - ling, dar - ling,

Chorus

stand   by me _____   oh, _____ stand   by

me.   Oh, stand,   stand by____ me, _____

stand ____   by me. _____

DAY TRIPPER

Words and Music by
JOHN LENNON and PAUL McCARTNEY

Melody:

Got a good rea - son

Intro

N.C.
(Guitar)

E

Verse

E

1. Got a good rea - son   for
2. She's a big teas - er.
3. Tried___ to please___ her.

tak - ing the eas - y way out.___
She took me half___ the way there.___
She on - ly played___ one night stands.___

Outro

Day trip - per.

Day trip - per, yeah._____

Day trip - per.

Day trip - per, yeah._____

CRAZY TRAIN

Words and Music by
OZZY OSBOURNE, RANDY RHOADS and BOB DAISLEY

Melody:

Cra - zy,

Intro

All aboard ha, ha, ha,...

Verse

1. Cra - zy,

but that's how it goes. _____

Mil - lions of peo - ple liv - ing as foes. _____

D　　　E　　　　F#m　　　　　　　　A　　　E

You've got - ta lis - ten to my

F#m　　　　　　D　　　E　　**Guitar Solo** F#m　　　E

words,＿＿＿＿ yeah,＿＿＿＿ yeah.＿＿＿＿

D　　　　　　　C#　　B　　A　　G#　F#m

F#m　　　　　E　D　　　　　C#　B　　A　　G#

1.　F#m　　　　　　　2.　F#m　　　　　3.　E

1.　　　　　　2. *D.S. al Coda*
F#m　　A5　E5　F#m　D　　E　D　　E

⊕ *Coda*　　　　　　　　　　　*Repeat and fade*

F#m　　　　　A　　E　　F#m　　　　D　　E

Ramblin' Man

Words and Music by
DICKEY BETTS

Melody:

Lord, I was born ___ a ram - blin' man.

Intro

Chorus

Lord I ___ was born ___ a ram - blin' man. ___

___ Try'n' to make a liv - in' and do - in' the best I ___

___ can. An' when it's time ___ for

leav - in' ___ I hope you'll un - der - stand, ___

Chorus

Lord, I___ was born___ a ram - blin'

man._____ Try'n' to make a liv - ing and

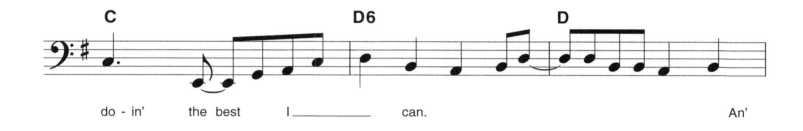

do - in' the best I_____ can. An'

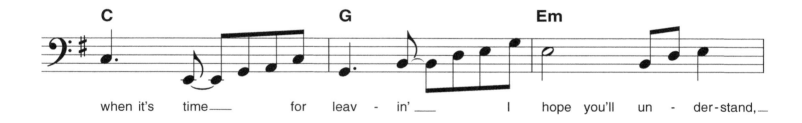

when it's time___ for leav - in'___ I hope you'll un - der-stand,___

To Coda

___ that I was born___ a ram - blin'

Interlude

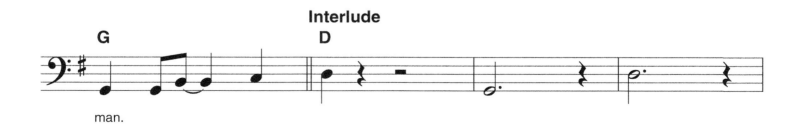

man.

Guitar Solo

D.S. al Coda

2. I'm

Coda

Outro-Chorus

man.

Lord, I _____ was born ___

Repeat and fade

___ a ram - blin' man. _____

38

JET AIRLINER

Words and Music by
PAUL PENA

Leav - in' on out ____ on the road. ____

Intro

Verse

1. Leav - in' on ____ out ____ on the road. ____
2. Good - bye to all ____ my friends at home, good - bye ____
3. Touch - in' down in New En - gland town, ____

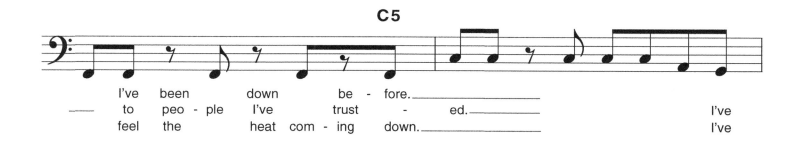

I've been down be - fore. ____
____ to peo - ple I've trust - ed. ____ I've
feel the heat com - ing down. ____ I've

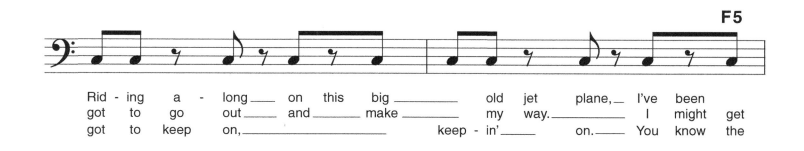

Rid - ing a - long ____ on this big ____ old jet plane, ____ I've been
got to go out ____ and ____ make ____ my way. ____ I might get
got to keep on, ____ keep - in' ____ on. ____ You know the

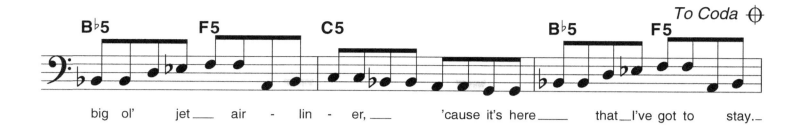

big ol' jet __ air - lin - er, ___ 'cause it's here___ that__I've got to stay.__

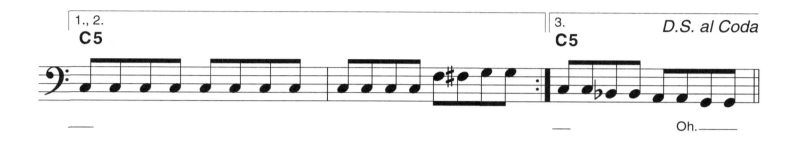

__ Oh.___

__ Yeah, yeah, yeah, yeah!___ Big ol' jet __ air - lin -

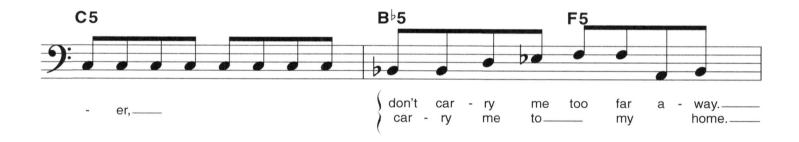

- er, ___

{ don't car - ry me too far a - way.___
{ car - ry me to___ my home.___

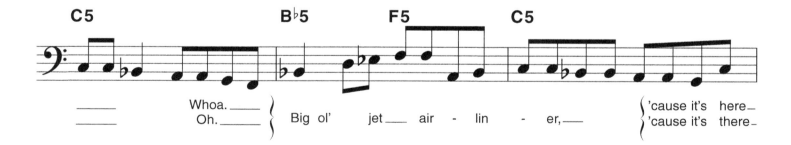

___ Whoa. ___ { Big ol' jet __ air - lin - er, ___ { 'cause it's here___
___ Oh. ___ { { 'cause it's there___

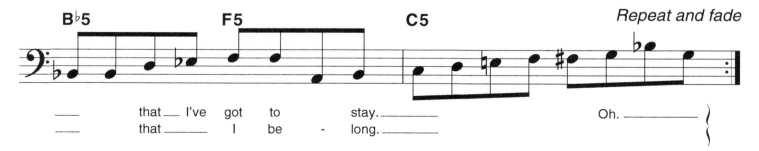

___ that __ I've got to stay.___ Oh. ___ {
___ that ___ I be - long.___

I Heard It Through the Grapevine

Words and Music by
NORMAN J. WHITFIELD and BARRETT STRONG

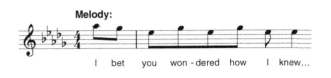

You could-'ve told _____ me your-self _____

_____ that you love _____ some-one else. _____ In - stead, I heard _____

Chorus

_____ it through the grape - vine. _____ Not much long - er would you be__ mine. _____

_____ Oh, I heard _____ it through the grape - vine. _____ And I'm just

a-bout to lose _____ my mind. ___ Hon -ey, hon -ey, well.

Outro   *Repeat and fade*

44

RHIANNON

Words and Music by
STEVIE NICKS

non. _____   Rhi - an   -

-                        non. _____   Rhi -

D.S. al Coda
(take 2nd ending)

an   -   non. _____

Coda

Outro-Chorus

Rhi - an   -

-                        non. _____

Repeat and fade

Rhi - an   -

Summer of '69

Words and Music by
BRYAN ADAMS and JIM VALLANCE

*Note played above the 12th fret.

YOU SHOOK ME

Written by
WILLIE DIXON and J. B. LENOIR

You shook me
I have a

1.

so ___ hard ___ ba-by,   ba - by, ___ ba - by, please ___ come

home. _____   2. I have a bird ___

2.

bird, ___   won't do noth-in', ___   oh, _____   oh, oh, ___

with-out a dia-mond ring. ___

Organ Solo

A7

E7

B7　　　　　　　　　　　A7　　　　　　　　　E　　Am　A♯°

Harmonica Solo

E7/B　　　B7　　　　E7

A7

E7

Guitar Solo

D.S. al Coda

3. You — know you

⊕ Coda

so   hard — ba-by,   you shook me   all — night — long. _____

Blue Suede Shoes

Words and Music by
CARL LEE PERKINS

DON'T BE CRUEL
(TO A HEART THAT'S TRUE)

Words and Music by
OTIS BLACKWELL and ELVIS PRESLEY

Melody:

You know I can be found ___

Intro
Shuffle
(Guitar)

1. You

Verse
C

know I can be found ___ sit - ting home all a -
2. Ba - by, if I made you mad for some - thing I might have said ___

C7   **F**

lone. If you can't come a - round at
___ please let's for - get my past at the

C   **Dm7** **G7**

least, please tel - e - phone. Don't be cruel _____ to a heart that's
fu - ture looks bright a - head. Don't be cruel _____ to a heart that's

true.   true.   I don't

Chorus

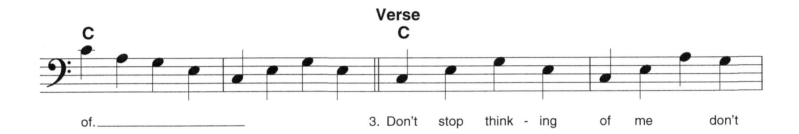

want no oth - er love,   ba - by, it's just you I'm think - ing

Verse

of._____   3. Don't stop think - ing of me don't

make me feel this way,   come on o - ver here and love me, you

know what I want you to say.   Don't be cruel _____ to a heart that's

LAY DOWN SALLY

**Words and Music by ERIC CLAPTON,
MARCY LEVY and GEORGE TERRY**

Melody:

There is noth-ing that___ is wrong___

Intro
Country Shuffle

§ **Verse**

A7

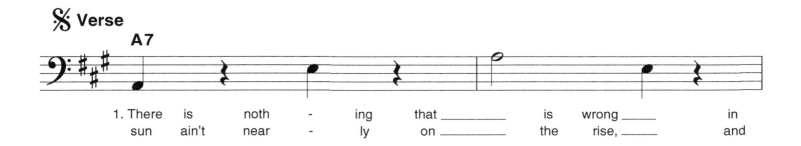

1. There is noth - ing that _____ is wrong _____ in
sun ain't near - ly on _____ the rise, _____ and

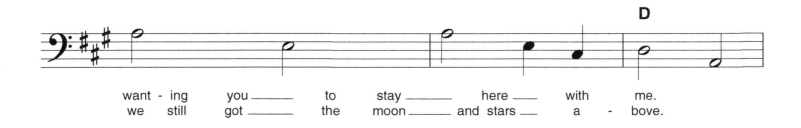

want - ing you _____ to stay _____ here _____ with me.
we still got _____ the moon _____ and stars _____ a - bove.

BAD, BAD LEROY BROWN

Words and Music by
JIM CROCE

Outro-Chorus

65

PRIDE AND JOY

Written by
STEVIE RAY VAUGHAN

Melody:

Well you've heard a - bout love...

Intro
Blues Shuffle

(Guitar)

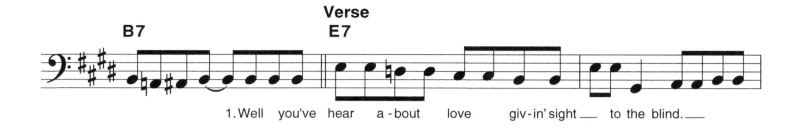

1. Well you've hear a-bout love giv-in' sight ___ to the blind. ___

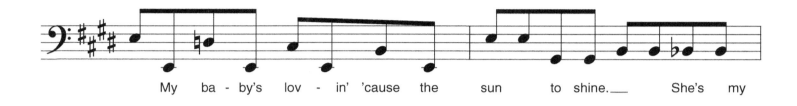

My ba-by's lov-in' 'cause the sun to shine. ___ She's my

sweet lit-tle thing. ___ She's my pride and joy. ___

She's my sweet lit-tle ba-by, I'm ___ her ___ lit-tle lov-er

boy. ___ 2. Yeah, I

love my ba-by my heart and ___ soul. ___ Love like ours won't

never grow ____ old. She's my sweet lit-tle thing. __

She's my pride and joy. ____

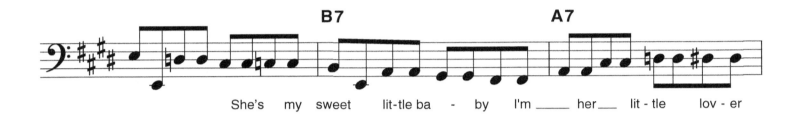

She's my sweet lit-tle ba - by I'm ____ her ___ lit - tle lov - er

Verse

boy. ____ 3. Yeah I love my la - dy she's

long and a lean. __ You mess with her, you'll see a

man get - tin' mean. __ She's my sweet lit - tle thing. __

She's my pride and joy. ___ She's my

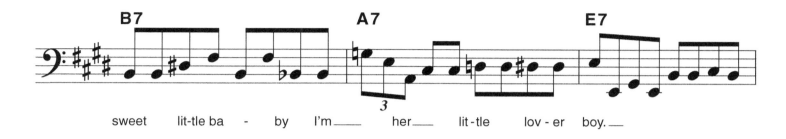

sweet lit-tle ba - by I'm ___ her ___ lit -tle lov - er boy. ___

Guitar Solo

MY GENERATION

Words and Music by
PETER TOWNSHEND

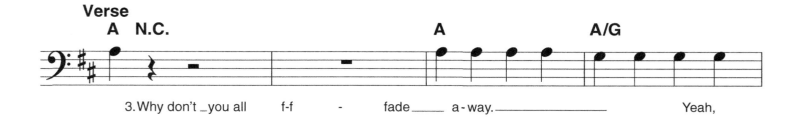

3. Why don't _ you all   f-f -   fade____ a-way._____   Yeah,

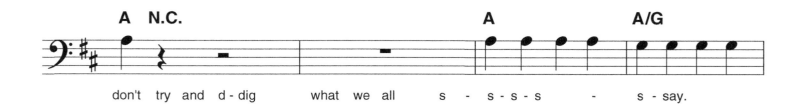

don't try and d - dig   what we all   s - s-s-s   -   s - say.

Not try-in' to cause big sen-sa - tion, just

talk-in' 'bout my g-gen-er-a - tion. ____ Ba - by, my __ gen-er-a-

Chorus

- tion, __ this is my __ gen-er-a - tion, ba - by. ____

____ My, my, ge - gen-er -

a - tion. My, my ooh, my, my.

Verse

4. Peo - ple try to put us d - down ____

HAL LEONARD BASS METHOD

METHOD BOOKS

by Ed Friedland

BOOK 1

Book 1 teaches: tuning; playing position; musical symbols; notes within the first five frets; common bass lines, patterns and rhythms; rhythms through eighth notes; playing tips and techniques; more than 100 great songs, riffs and examples; and more! The audio includes 44 full-band tracks for demonstration or play-along.

00695067 Book Only.................................. $7.99
00695068 Book/Online Audio............................ $12.99

BOOK 2

Book 2 continues where Book 1 left off and teaches: the box shape; moveable boxes; notes in fifth position; major and minor scales; the classic blues line; the shuffle rhythm; tablature; and more!

00695069 Book Only.................................. $7.99
00695070 Book/Online Audio............................ $12.99

BOOK 3

With the third book, progressing students will learn more great songs, riffs and examples; sixteenth notes; playing off chord symbols; slap and pop techniques; hammer-ons and pull-offs; playing different styles and grooves; and more.

00695071 Book Only.................................. $7.99
00695072 Book/Online Audio............................ $12.99

COMPOSITE

This money-saving edition contains Books 1, 2 and 3.
00695073 Book Only.................................. $17.99
00695074 Book/Online Audio............................ $24.99

DVD

Play your favorite songs in no time with this DVD! Covers: tuning, notes in first through third position, rhythms through eighth notes, fingerstyle and pick playing, 4/4 and 3/4 time, and more! Includes 6 full songs and on-screen music notation. 68 minutes.

00695849 DVD $19.95

BASS FOR KIDS

by Chad Johnson

Bass for Kids is a fun, easy course that teaches children to play bass guitar faster than ever before. Popular songs such as "Crazy Train," "Every Breath You Take," "A Hard Day's Night" and "Wild Thing" keep kids motivated, and the clean, simple page layouts ensure their attention remains focused on one concept at a time.

00696449 Book/Online Audio $12.99

REFERENCE BOOKS

BASS SCALE FINDER

by Chad Johnson

Learn to use the entire fretboard with the *Bass Scale Finder*. This book contains over 1,300 scale diagrams for the most important 17 scale types.

00695781 6" x 9" Edition.......................................$7.99
00695778 9" x 12" Edition.....................................$7.99

BASS ARPEGGIO FINDER

by Chad Johnson

This extensive reference guide lays out over 1,300 arpeggio shapes. 28 different qualities are covered for each key, and each quality is presented in four different shapes.

00695817 6" x 9" Edition.......................................$7.99
00695816 9" x 12" Edition.....................................$7.99

MUSIC THEORY FOR BASSISTS

by Sean Malone

Acclaimed bassist and composer Sean Malone will explain the written language of music, using easy-to-understand terms and concepts, diagrams, and much more. The audio provides 96 tracks of examples, demonstrations, and play-alongs.

00695756 Book/Online Audio $17.99

STYLE BOOKS

BASS LICKS

by Ed Friedland

This comprehensive supplement to any bass method will help students learn over 200 great bass licks, lines and grooves in many rhythmic styles. *Bass Licks* illustrates how simple melodic patterns can become the springboard for group improvisation or the foundation of a song.

00696035 Book/Online Audio $14.99

BASS LINES

by Matt Scharfglass

500 expertly written bass lines, riffs and fills in a wide variety of musical genres are included in this comprehensive collection to help players expand their bass vocabulary. The examples cover many tempos, keys and feels, and include easy bass lines for beginners on up to advanced riffs for more experienced bassists.

00148194 Book/Online Audio $19.99

BLUES BASS

by Ed Friedland

Learn to play studying the songs of B.B. King, Stevie Ray Vaughan, Muddy Waters, Albert King, the Allman Brothers, T-Bone Walker, and many more. Learn riffs from blues classics including: Born Under a Bad Sign • Hideaway • Hoochie Coochie Man • Killing Floor • Pride and Joy • Sweet Home Chicago • The Thrill Is Gone • and more.

00695870 Book/Online Audio $14.99

COUNTRY BASS

by Glenn Letsch

21 songs, including: Act Naturally • Boot Scootin' Boogie • Crazy • Honky Tonk Man • Love You Out Loud • Luckenbach, Texas (Back to the Basics of Love) • No One Else on Earth • Ring of Fire • Southern Nights • Streets of Bakersfield • Whose Bed Have Your Boots Been Under? • and more.

00695928 Book/Online Audio $17.99

FRETLESS BASS

by Chris Kringel

18 songs, including: Bad Love • Continuum • Even Flow • Everytime You Go Away • Hocus Pocus • I Could Die for You • Jelly Roll • King of Pain • Kiss of Life • Lady in Red • Tears in Heaven • Very Early • What I Am • White Room • more.

00695850...$19.99

FUNK BASS

by Chris Kringel

This is your complete guide to learning the basics of grooving and soloing funk bass. Songs include: Can't Stop • I'll Take You There • Let's Groove • Stay • What Is Hip • and more.

00695792 Book/Online Audio...........................$22.99

R&B BASS

by Glenn Letsch

This book/audio pack uses actual classic R&B, Motown, soul and funk songs to teach you how to groove in the style of James Jamerson, Bootsy Collins, Bob Babbitt, and many others. The 19 songs include: For Once in My Life • Knock on Wood • Mustang Sally • Respect • Soul Man • Stand by Me • and more.

00695823 Book/Online Audio $17.99

ROCK BASS

by Sean Malone

This book/audio pack uses songs from a myriad of rock genres to teach the key elements of rock bass. Includes: Another One Bites the Dust • Beast of Burden • Money • Roxanne • Smells like Teen Spirit • and more.

00695801 Book/Online Audio...........................$21.99

SUPPLEMENTARY SONGBOOKS

These great songbooks correlate with Books 1-3 of the *Hal Leonard Bass Method*, giving students great songs to play while they're still learning! The audio tracks include great accompaniment and demo tracks.

EASY POP BASS LINES

20 great songs that students in Book 1 can master. Includes: Come as You Are • Crossfire • Great Balls of Fire • Imagine • Surfin' U.S.A. • Takin' Care of Business • Wild Thing • and more.

00695810 Book Only..................................$9.99
00695809 Book/Online Audio..........................$15.99

MORE EASY POP BASS LINES

20 great songs for Level 2 students. Includes: Bad, Bad Leroy Brown • Crazy Train • I Heard It Through the Grapevine • My Generation • Pride and Joy • Ramblin' Man • Summer of '69 • and more.

00695819 Book Only.................................$12.99
00695818 Book/Online Audio..........................$16.99

EVEN MORE EASY POP BASS LINES

20 great songs for Level 3 students, including: ABC • Another One Bites the Dust • Brick House • Come Together • Higher Ground • Iron Man • The Joker • Sweet Emotion • Under Pressure • more.

00695821 Book $9.99
00695820 Book/Online Audio..........................$16.99

Visit Hal Leonard online at
www.halleonard.com

Prices, contents and availability subject to change without notice.
Some products may not be available outside of U.S.A.